Before the Night Wakes You

poems by

Len Lawson

Finishing Line Press
Georgetown, Kentucky

Before the Night Wakes You

For Shay

Copyright © 2017 by Len Lawson
ISBN 978-1-63534-124-9 First Edition
All rights reserved under International and Pan-American Copyright Conventions.
No part of this book may be reproduced in any manner whatsoever without written permission from the publisher, except in the case of brief quotations embodied in critical articles and reviews.

ACKNOWLEDGMENTS

"Deep Sea", a Pushcart Prize nominee, and "Uncle J's Blues" appeared in *The Petigru Review* anthology
"Smashing Bottles" was shortlisted by *Berfrois Magazine* for its 2014 inaugural poetry prize
"I Write My Body Eclectic" appeared in *[PANK]* Magazine.
"[Uneasy] Dreams of a Presidential Hopeful" appeared in *Connotation Press*.
"Traffic Stop" appeared in *pluck! A Journal of Affrilachian Arts and Culture*
"Google search for *black lives matter*" appeared in *Winter Tangerine Review*
"I Hate My Own Breath" appeared in *Pittsburgh Poetry Review*.
An excerpt of "Pages from the Coward's Playbook" appeared in *Jasper Magazine*
"Feel the Vibration" appeared in *Yellow Chair Review*
"Church Fan" appeared in *Drunk in a Midnight Choir*
"Praise Song for the Waters" appeared in the *Mississippi Review*
"Manhood Dreams" was accepted into the Hope Paige Designs 2016 *Anthology on Loss*
"Separation" and "Briefcase of Little Tortures" appeared in *Up the Staircase Quarterly*

Publisher: Leah Maines

Editor: Christen Kincaid

Cover Art: https://commons.wikimedia.org/wiki/File:Henri_Rousseau_010.jpg

Author Photo: Michael Dantzler Photography

Cover Design: Elizabeth Maines

Printed in the USA on acid-free paper.
Order online: www.finishinglinepress.com
also available on amazon.com

Author inquiries and mail orders:
Finishing Line Press
P. O. Box 1626
Georgetown, Kentucky 40324
U. S. A.

Table of Contents

Deep Sea 1

Uncle J's Blues 2

Smashing Battles 3

Middle Passage 4

I Write My Body Eclectic 5

[Uneasy] Dreams of a Presidential Hopeful 6

I Want to Play the Race Card in a Game of Spades 8

Traffic Stop 10

Picking Powerball Numbers 11

Google search for *black lives matter* 12

I Hate My Own Breath 14

Page from the Coward's Playbook 15

Feel the Vibration: Marky Mark & the Funky Bunch,
    A Retrospective 17

Church Fan 19

Praise Song for the Waters 22

The Invitation 25

The Waiting Room 27

Manhood *Dreams* 29

Separation 30

Briefcase of Little Tortures 31

To my Creator, God, my Heavenly Father, I believe, and no one will ever change that.

To my late father, you are always near. To my mother, sister, stepfather, and grandmother, these words have become what I was placed in the world to do. Thank you for being in my corner.

To friends and family, the support means everything. To anyone who has taken a genuine interest in my work, I am humbled that these words have touched you.

Deep Sea

> *Deep calleth unto deep at the noise of Thy waterspouts: all*
> *Thy waves and Thy billows are gone over me.*
> *Psalm 42:7; The Holy Bible, King James Version*

Eyes still breathe under water
Just through prisms like marbles
They see the world as ocean

Galaxies of vision
Beckoning sky and sea
Heaven and deep

Ascending and descending
I thought my eyes drowned
Staring at Daddy's body

On that ER bed
My sister's eyes too
Mama never reached out to save our eyes

She also never said if Daddy's eyes
Reached out for us before returning to the deep
I haven't blinked to find out

Uncle J's Blues

He had two daughters
seven years apart
no son yet

lost his finger and bike in a
motorcycle accident
still had his white Mustang Cobra

took off his cool before Daddy's wake
long enough to wear me as
his black leather vest

walking up Hunters Chapel Road
peering down at me through
aviator sunglasses

It wasn't about how many beers
he and Daddy knocked back or
how many they'd never knock back again

I was the boy he never had that day
I thought I became his phantom finger too
No, I became the nub that would

never grow back

Smashing Bottles

We weren't in a gang. We weren't thieves or drug dealers. We weren't even gifted or artistic. We were blameless in our pursuit of play. None of us ever even wondered how the bottles got there—not to threaten the integrity and innocence of our game. We could have staked out the woods and caught those drunken hunters red-handed. Then, maybe one of us would have gotten shot by a hunting rifle—right between the eyes of our black faces in the chilly darkness. And maybe those hunters would have scrambled to the spot to find another dead black boy in the wilderness. And maybe they would have left him there in his blood to stain the woods with his innocence. And maybe we would have found him and brought him to his mama and family. And maybe the news would travel to that spot the next day. And maybe we'd've told them our story: that we were looking for drunken hunters in the woods to stop littering our Mother Nature. Maybe the killer would have been found. Maybe he'd've been questioned—maybe arrested, maybe indicted, maybe arraigned and sent to trial. And maybe—just maybe—the drunken hunting white bastard would have gone to jail for manslaughter—or even murder if he saw us in the woods that night before shooting. Then, we could have smashed those bottles in the streets for a cause—maybe would have gone to jail, maybe would have been shot and killed by police in those streets. But we weren't activists or martyrs. We were black boys, and we just wanted to play.

Middle Passage

Praise the river and the ocean weeps red
Flowing to estuaries of nightmares
Rivers cleanse bodies while oceans hide them
The term freshwater empties them of guilt
Show me a bridge and I'll show you coffins
Which do you think tells Black stories better
I celebrate drowners more than divers
Because drowners will reach the bottom first
Forgive me, the black bodies did not drown
They were dead before touching the water
Slave ships would prefer never to look down
They dream winds filling their sails without blame
Beyond the mirror ripples and red waves
Black bodies in water form a Dead Sea

I Write My Body Eclectic
After Walt Whitman.

    I, too, sing my body

                              I sing classical
           the slave auction was the finest opera

tropical storm of my black body
        fresh off the auction block to
bury its throat / its diaphragm / the screech and holler of
                                         its crushed voice box
in the acoustics of a white sepulcher plantation

              Inhale this body's rain
                        husky with peeled and licked sores
    Winds ripe with skin allergies
        Slave-exhaled clouds plush with so much hair

              hair singing the gospel on every blade of skin
           Jesus be Rapunzel's kinky natural hair tsunami

        Every thunder is an open wound
              Clap!
Ripped from bloodlines by shackles
              Clap!
Stripped of tribal garb for ruffled blouses
              Clap!
Dipped in the acid rain of race

        I sing…no I clap back!

                        with rhythm and rhyme and
    beat and box and turn and table and microphone and
cussing and harmony and blues and jazz and rock and   hip and hop and
beat machines and engineers and
                the sweetest soulful Sound Cloud
    over the Gulf to calm the tropical skies

My melody pumps black blood on wax for
        the ancestors to rain dance and
appropriators to pray guilty tears to

[Uneasy] Dreams of a Presidential Hopeful
> *As Gregor Samsa awoke one morning from uneasy dreams he found himself transformed in his bed into a gigantic insect.*
> —Franz Kafka, "The Metamorphosis"

                Unholy percussion
Hum of savages
      calling forth
           ravens
                panthers
                      black widows [deadly by their grief]

Breaths of the   burns of little girls in churches
                      fan-sliced faces of drowned boys
                      bullet holes of brown boys
                      caves in a star-smacked and blood-striped flag

                Smoldering around their necks and on their forearms
                      The 14th & 15th Amendments
                      The gasping last words of Eric Garner
                      Bible verses about masters and servants
                            used to hang ancestors daily

                spilling out of   jungle brush
                                          Mammy's kitchen
                                          slave quarters
                          neglected segregated shadows
                          affirmative action wrung dry
                          death's wincing grip
                Out of
        time
the dark lapse between breaths that history
                      and its autographed books ignore

They come with signs
  war cries
  fists punching Godward to thunder the skies
                    louder
                    darker
                    angrier
          Addicted to a candidate's   nightmares
                                            nausea
                                          terror

                                        trickling sweat as euphemism
                                        for trembling tears

In their own dreams
White
[Not heavenly white but]
              The gash of lightning
         ruthless calculated aggression of clouds
         gall and sludge of milk
         repugnance of white lies graffitied across their psyches
         longsuffering of black words on white pages wrapped in
              black covers tagged with the word *Holy*
White fingers on black triggers
White sheets over black souls
Whitewashed words rolling over blackened tongues
         Breaths of   zebras
                           pandas
                              killer whales
                                   Killer whale
                                   Kill her whale
                                   Kill her well
                                        but
                                   Say her name
                                   Sandra Bland
                                   Never forget
                                   Never erase
                                   The subconscious
              is a funhouse   mirror   Bizarre
how dreams share their vapors with fog
How the brain is shaped like a cloud
         Like dust
Like ashes   when   filled   with   rain...
              I forgot this is a poem about trying to sleep
         which the sound of rain will help
                   Unless the ancestors'   [unborn]
                                            [stillborn]
                                            [still unborn]
                           sons and daughters
                        provide the dancing

I Want to Play the Race Card in a Game of Spades

The moment broadcast like the World Series of Spades
Flat screens fade to black worldwide
Not a test of the Emergency Broadcast System
Emergency signals muted by a shadow of four centuries

No colors as prison bars on the screens
The absence of color and all that
If this had been an actual emergency
Then every card in every deck in every game

Worldwide would be assimilated like Agent Smith in
The Matrix Revolutions and the One would be
Black by his skin not just by his suit and by his shades and
By his guns and by his choice of mentors and

The esophagus of the card would
Swallow you whole while you swallow
Whole a shadow of four centuries. The card
Won't be available to pull from the deck

Black all over with nothing else on it
Nothing but that smooth matte finish
The absence of light and all that
You awaken and tell yourself

You must have blacked out for a second after its cloak covers you
Your black pupils press their palms together and
Pray to Hannibals and Shaka Zulus and actual black Cleopatras
When this totem of lost souls reveals itself

Won't be dealt or shuffled or flipped or cut or
Dangled between the valleys of my fingers or
Fanned between royalty and bloodletting
Your lips will curl between your teeth when

I use it and you won't be able to say
Hey, all cards matter, after it sucks into black hole oblivion
Your whole hand of cards, your whole stack of books
The score of statistics you've tallied

Your possibles hoping to be weak trumps that might slip in
To scoop up an unsuspecting book when no one is looking
No, there will be a moment of silence when it appears
For every other time that it could have

And should have been used
Its holiness too rich for my hands
Crowning my forehead for the entire game
Just so you know I can use it whenever I please

You won't have to search the Mayas and Martins in my eyes for its coming
For when it births its dimension from the guilt of your subconscious
You will say, think, hear, or feel nothing. You'll be as lonely as its inception
You'll become as soulless and wretched as I for having to use it!

It is the only partner I'll need in this game
It is the game. It is the players. It is the rules.
Matter of fact, I want to use this card in War and Rummy
And Poker and Hearts and every other game you've created

And for business and for credit and for my calling
My birth and death certificate
It is universal. It begs. It cries.
It is desperate for its destiny to be played

Traffic Stop

See yourself as messiah
Save your sins from yourself

Watch the diamonds of your grace can-can single file
from the red and blue lights before your concussion sets in

Let the glaze of fresh crimson across your face trickle sweet
down your tongue coating your words with impeccable scripture

You are the Second Adam. Your exposed
boxers are what his fig leaves could never do

Your patience must shatter your crown of thorns
They must be planks javelined into the eyes of their whites

Feel no cuffs slicing away at your livelihood
just faith to save the world in God's time

It will soon be over. Ignore the motor oil and fresh black
asphalt filling your nostrils as your face penetrates the street

Arise, black golden child, and sin no more
Your humiliation is now the salt and light to cover

the earth because this time he's letting you
off with only a warning. Hosanna.

Picking Powerball Numbers

Quick! Pick the numbers for the distance
between each dead black body in the streets

Quick! Pick the number of cigarettes Eric Garner was holding
Market value for the smoke that will whisper the last words of his breath

Quick! Pick the seconds to identify a black boy's toy gun as a weapon of mass destruction
Quick! Pick how many of Freddie Gray's bones were left unbroken

You could play
                        Friendship 9
                                       Charleston 9
                                                        Jena 6

How about the 9 more black boys that will be
killed in this nation by police than white boys

Maybe you should use the number of letters in each of their names

        Laquan McDonald   ...14
        Trayvon Martin   ...13
        Michael Brown   ...12
        Freddie Gray   ...11
        Eric Garner   ...10
        Tamir Rice   ...9

...Stop! How many more must die before the letters add up to 0

Scraping the numbers off tragedies could earn
millions but if I get gunned down for stretching

this black body on the world's canvas before you can
collect then burn every dollar bill in the same street

where my blood will ascend to the heavens in a
vapor like you're counting down to the new year

and my body is your final shout

Google search for *black lives matter*

Did you mean <u>slaves</u>
Searching instead for <u>indentured servants, cheerful workers</u>

black lives matter   Orangeburg Massacre
                                  Kent State
                                  Los Angeles Riots
                                  Ferguson
                                  Baltimore
                                  North Charleston
                                  too many bodies to name in a poem

Did you mean <u>Michael Jackson Oprah Beyonce</u>
Searching instead for <u>famous black bodies that transcend color</u>

black lives matter   when killed by cops
                                  when body cams fail
                                  when cell phones stay charged
                                  when terror is not imported but a natural resource
                                  when   white lives need votes
                                                      white lives say so
                                                      white sheets cast shadows
                                                      white doesn't mean holy

Did you mean <u>niggers, Nigga</u>?
Searching instead for <u>your transfusion, your transplant, your ripped-off
                                culture, your guilty pleasure</u>

black lives matter   when black mothers go bankrupt planning black
                                  baby funerals
                                  when black girls go up flag poles and come down
                                  superheroes

                    when black bodies   speak out
                                                jog in the suburbs
                                                fit a criminal description
                                                invade white privilege

                                    go silent in jail cells
                                    get detained by swarms of police

Did you mean <u>buffoons</u>?
Searching instead for <u>black face</u>

        black *lives*   in American shadows
                                 in the center of white pupils
                                 in white bloodlines   Thomas Jefferson
                                 in between white lines   dark city streets
                                 in the bottom of crab barrels   black people
                                 syndrome
                                 in color charts not skin tone
                                 hue and spectrum
                                 in wherever black damn well pleases
                                 you mad bro
                                 sorry not sorry

Did you mean <u>minstrel, coon, jigaboo, spook, and the names we don't
        know you use</u> <u>because you say them in private?</u>

Searching instead for <u>Nubian, Umoja, Ujima, melanin, ebony</u>
                          <u>the bubbling brown sugar you ignore when you just
                          want to use the word</u> *ghetto* <u>to wipe yourself clean of
                          your chain letter history</u>

black lives *matter*   the air you breathe
                               the earth you stand on
                               the universe you praise
                               your god's heaven

                               big bang
                               big black bang
                               big black loud bang
                               big black loud angry BANG

I Hate My Own Breath

I want to sell bottles of this breath as an aphrodisiac to cowards with badges and cowards with hoods and cowards who whimper to wear my black skin like a lion pelt to the freshest party in some fake Holly-hood where whiteness is the gateway feigning the quartz below the pearls below the diamonds below the stars praising the holy heaven that is a black man's teeth / wisdom of a coon / jewelry / accessories to outfit manifest destiny / poking holes in earlobes as a gift outright / can they hear the spirituals whistling through bicuspids / and nibbling on flesh around necks / can their throats bob up and down on the swinging noose of their Adam's apple / My breath will be the smoothest scented gem they wear, but they'll never even ask me for the alchemy of the potion / It'll be ripped from my esophagus behind the midnight jig of a trigger finger without a decadent morning after breath kiss goodbye which is why I hate this black breath scent under my nostrils romancing and awaiting the fame

Page from the Coward's Playbook

Nine churches in the South were burned inexplicably in the summer of 2015. There have been no criminals brought to justice. Six occurred in the fall near St. Louis with no arrests.

There are over 1,000 white supremacist organizations registered in the United States. The Ku Klux Klan, most prominent and boisterous of the organizations, contains twelve public chapters across the U.S.

I.

When anything does not go your way, blame, burn, or murder the meek and disenfranchised. Any of these is acceptable, but all of the above will ease the most pain.

II.

Take your proverbial ball and go home when your rightful demands are not met, and by ball we mean your entire state.

III.

White sheets bring you closer to an all-white god in an all-white heaven with all-white angels occupied by all-white whites and we-can't-even-see-anything-because-it-is-so-white-up-here white and white white white white white…

IV.

White cloth will not make you sweat as much on hot nights in the country walking down dirt roads to spook houses with blazing torch in one hand and foaming, barking Doberman in the other as long as you keep air moving through your suit by turning the dog loose, tossing the torch through the nearest window when you get to the coon's house (preferably a bedroom window), then punching and kicking them coons repeatedly after they run out the house so that you can beat the heat.

V.

It will be acceptable to forget the Scriptures we stand for when you come up against crimes (i.e. murder, arson, assault, battery, home invasion, destruction of property, carrying unlawful fire arms). The law will not apply to you when your hood goes on.

VI.

Scapegoats for setting churches on fire include lightning, faulty wiring, cigarettes, "Dem coons just make it too hot in there from all that yelling and dancing," "Somebody left that gas can outside the building," and, of course, "Niggers always lie."

VII.

Infiltrating and occupying positions like police officer, fireman, lawyer, chief of police, sheriff, judge, jury, mayor, senator, governor, and president will ensure the acquittal of our brothers in crimes mentioned in V. If coons are in these positions in the event of one of our arrests, refer back to I.

VIII.

When these coons begin thinking they have power, when they think they can mobilize, boycott, speak ill of our heritage and the foundations of our pure and prestigious brotherhood, and especially when they start marrying our daughters, gather at the most sacred monuments of our forefathers, refer to yourselves as sons of history, hold your stars and bars high for all white heaven to see, and prepare to secede from the Union again, ignite the race war again, and don't get no nigger bloodstains or bodily fluids on your gleaming, white glory suit—so help you God.

Feel the Vibration: Marky Mark & the Funky Bunch, a Retrospective

[Raspy, fake gangsta voice] *Yeahhhh!*

Abs glistening. Boxer briefs biting down hard on his waist. Ball cap low to the west.

C'mon, c'mon! Feel it, feel it! We ate it up like white chocolate.

Because he worked out in a pseudo jail cell for a quasi-hardcore video. Because of the mock training scenes stolen from the LL Cool J "Mama Said Knock You Out" video.

Because we tolerated the exploitation of Loleatta Holloway, a black woman singing her soul out like Aretha, in the shadows on the screen.

Because we even looked the other way at the lame ass name for his "crew", taken from the reject pile for garage band names.

We should see Mark Wahlberg and C & C Music Factory's David Cole, the lite version (not literally) of Ice-T, square off in a ring with both Loleatta and Martha Wash, whose throat was ripped out and placed in a skinnier black body in C & C's "Sweat" video, belting out their anthems in each corner.

Wahlberg would get the win because he could call out Vanilla Ice, Snow, or even his protégé of fake hip hop swag John Cena to give him a microphone of white gold to smash Ice-T Lite in the head with when the ref conveniently would not be looking.

(Ice-T Lite couldn't get any real niggas to assist him.)

The Funky Bunch and the Music Factory would brawl out of the arena to the streets *West Side Story* style.

When the smoke would clear, the two soulful divas would be left standing in the center of the ring for a clapback rendition of the real Negro National Anthem "Live Every Voice".

But even after winning, Mark would still hang up his briefs (or be hung up by his briefs) because maybe Suge Knight would get to him like he did Vanilla Ice and dangle him over a balcony and say, *If you say the words* Feel the Vibration *no more goddam time, Imma steal the souls from your kids and eat you and your no-talent-having-ass family alive!*

Abruptly, Wahlberg put on some clothes and became a fake brother to Andre 3000 and Tyrese, a (real) fake fighter, and friend to a talking brown bear who can say just about any ethnic slur in a quest to be "real"…We're still licking our fingers.

Black, yellow, red, brown
Feel the vibration (of appropriation)!

Church Fan
    —or I should say—church fanatic

                              1.
    Martin Luther King on the front in suspended animation deeply troubled by the congregation

            funeral home awaiting them on the back

Martin Luther King outside the church at the front awaiting their arrival to the Promise Land

the funeral home director under a canopy in the back deeply troubled by their animated march to the grave

                              2.
    white jesus patient with bated knuckles on the front

    funeral home locked on the back

Real Jesus patiently knocking with bruised knuckles and pierced hands at the front door

funeral home canopy fanning the dead in the teeming graveyard out the back door

                              3.
    fan waving in a holy ghost haze in front of faces dripping with discount makeup and White Diamonds wrestling with the aroma of fried chicken cooling on the stove for Sunday or midweek revival

fans waving their hands in the face of God while their rain dance wears the plush out of the velvet carpet dripping with sins from last night / from last hour / from last minute / from last I checked there are no white diamonds on the pearly gates so my spiritual calisthenics / my holy yoga / won't facetime with God on Sundays or midweek

4.

when you realize the funeral home made those fans to advertise arrangements for your death

yes, for your death because someone has to make those arrangements for you

while you try to get a few DM's into the King's throne room of prayer but the throne room already has your death marked

so any arrangements advertised by a cardboard portrait on a stick only reminds the throne room of your impending death certificate

and in essence the entire church is dead and every fan in it so that the stick fans the flames of hell in the face of God

when you realize on Saturday night you could have been a homeless-man-you-passed-on-Martin Luther-King-Blvd fan

or a confused-gang-member-you-narrowly-escaped-on-Martin-Luther-King-Blvd fan

or a domestic-violence-victim-you-pitied-because-of-her-bruised-blotchy-cheeks-where-hairs-have-been-yanked-out-and-her-thorned-forehead-where-her-crown-once-lay-and-doubled-over-because-of-her-pierced-side-curled-up-in-an-alley-on-Martin-Luther-King-Blvd fan

or a hungry-child fan or hungry-for-a-child-to-be-hungry-for-her-own-hunger-for-destiny-so-she-can-get-off-Martin-Luther-King-Blvd fan

> but you decided to be hungry for pastor's robe and church lights and cameras and action action-action-we-need-more-action-in-these-streets preaching thunderbolted down from Mount Pulpit

5.

so you wave your dollars beckoning the collection plate
like a fan while the band plays soft jazz and singers avoid the name

of God by shimmying through contemporary inspirational lyrics

and you wave your baby in your arms like a fan at the front of the altar to sacrifice another life at the foot of the mountain

and you wave your body between this world and the next like a fan every Sunday then go home to your broken beaten break beat beaten broken reality

and you turn on football and watch for hours like a fan and when the game is over and the stadium lights go out you sit in darkness and you wait for heaven

and you wonder now who the hell is ever going to be a fan of me

Praise Song for the Waters
After the South Carolina Thousand-year Flood Event

praise for the dams that
would not hold

praise for the miracle when the waters
walked on dry land

praise for the liberation of
the word dry

praise for Nikky Haley's mantra
after the waters walked down on air

We. Will. Get. Through. This.

praise for getting through
not   passing through

not   wading through
not even   living   through

praise for the 48 hours straight the waters
ran their marathon through the bowels of
ol' Palmetto State

praise the desperate souls who drove out
to cheer them and got swept up
in their tailwind

praise the F-150
praise the V-8 engine
praise the roaring motor and
the booming horn and
the trips to AutoZone to make it
even louder but silenced
in its race with the waters

ran a close second
to death
dead in the water

praise for the dead
praise the getting up
the getting up and out
the early morning resurrections

praise the gathering
of the waterbed caskets
to see the faces of the dead
one more time

praise for faces
with smiles after cries
praise the crying face of Carolina

praise other hands
that wipe our faces

praise other dry hands
on our wet faces

praise for the coronation of
the word dry

praise for the waters in bottles
and more bottles
and cases of bottles
wrapped on pallets
stacked in every corner
delivered by once dry hands

the waters always win

We are still wet with
fear of the waters

We are still wet with
stories of the waters

Our souls have grown
wet like the waters

praise for the echo
the infinity
the second, third, and fourth coming of
the word *dry*

The Invitation

I saw my picture in the paper
chalk outline expression
worst tape-up line ever
hair running jagged on my forehead
like a runaway slave

my body swinging
between soul and spirit

if it were my last night
surrounded by sons of the confederacy
I'd be that black boy who
should have known better than to go down
into a snake hole looking for
validation in venom

laughing politely
at their nigger jokes

my best friend already telling me,
I know I ain't going down there
to get lynched

I saw no end to the color lines
carnage / cold-blooded killing in
every tongue lash of
I don't see color
I don't have a problem with y'all
I like black people

I saw no avengers
no millions marching down Main Street
with my picture on 2 x 4's
no candlelight on the steps of city hall
no flowers bowing in prayer
no Snickers bars and Yoohoo bottles
left outside the county library
one of my favorite spots

the moment fading on the calendar
year after year into a forgotten
abyss of black boy names
crowded under the bonfire of
burning crosses

so when those boys I sat with
in every class
eight hours a day
ate with while hearing the word *nigger* at the lunch table
played at recess with as an accessory to any game
asked me to grace one of their
drunken Friday night parties with my blackness

I smiled politely with the bonfire flame
and fear of Kunta Kinte in my eyes and said

But who's gonna carry my body
back to Mama

The Waiting Room

when you storm off from the den couch into the bathroom and sit with
elbows on knees and skinny fingers clinched together after your mama
breaks the news to you and your older sister that your daddy just died

you sit on the cold toilet seat at the back of the house and wait and maybe
you count out loud

you wait for your daddy to poke his head through the bathroom window
and jerk you by the arm and yell *Whatchu doin there, boy* and you delight
in his skills as a master trickster

you wait and maybe count out loud but you don't cry

you wait for your mama to break the news to you and your sister much
better than saying *Well, y'all, your daddy didn't make it*
you wait for details, you wait for what took the god out of his own world,
you wait for the why

you wait and maybe you count out loud but you don't cry unless
somebody calls your name to come back out to the den

you wait to understand how the man feigned perfect health two hours
before when you returned home from school and asked if he needed
anything because you knew he was sick, how the man lay on his back
in bed and reported he needed nothing, how he sat in bed and waited
for death, how he didn't trust your nappy headed, bony, 12-year-old
frame with the truth of his condition, how he risked his own life for your
beautiful, precious innocence in his eyes

you wait and maybe you count out loud but you don't cry unless
somebody calls your name to come back out to the den for pizza waiting
in the kitchen

you wait because you're mad at your sister's eyes for trembling tears directly in your face like a staring contest that you just lost because you stomped away

you wait and maybe you count out loud because that's how people show they're mad but you definitely don't cry unless somebody calls your name to come back out to the den for pizza waiting in the kitchen with the biggest laugh they ever made shaking your family tree because nothing like this should ever happen to a child

but then you run out of numbers to count because counting is boring and you remember you don't cry for this world's evil and you can't sift through your shock to smell pepperoni and cheese at the front of the house and no matter who calls your name it won't be daddy and when they show you his body on the ER bed, you will trade your dry eyes for your sister's blurry ones

so you open the bathroom door to step through the veil daddy tried to protect you from and you tell that gorgeous black body of his waiting for you on that ER bed

the wait is over

Manhood Dreams

He died when I was a boy.

Decades later, I still experience his death in dreams, but in each, I am a grown man. In one, I run away from my family and do not attend the funeral. During their worship service, I hide in a different church where no one knows or recognizes me. Eventually friends and family find me there. Was I a man or still just a boy?

In another dream, a man-sized me is in the middle of a little league baseball game. I round second base to make a triple, but the throw to third stops my progress. Every kid on the field and both coaches converge to tag me out in a rundown. When they finally do, I look to the stands searching for Daddy. He isn't there. To me, I was still just a boy.

I am also a man in a dream where I am driving Daddy's big, bright, red Ford pick-up. Where its proportions dwarfed me as a kid, now it fits just right, with my hands on the steering wheel and him beside me in the passenger seat. We pull into a gas station and when two men come up to service our vehicle we get out of the truck. Together, we stare into an open frontier that looks like one of those 1940's picturesque movie scenes. We just stand there quietly, two men side by side. It is the best moment of my life—in a dream.

Today, I tended my father's grave site. We had a good conversation. I said, "You were a better man than I could ever hope to be. You provided for a family and still cared for your elderly mother after her husband's death. You were a dad to sons, nephews, and fathers. I am not yet a man. When I die, I want to be buried right beside you so that you can finish teaching me."

Then, I asked why he keeps showing up in my dreams. His response was the same as always: no answer. In death as in life, his presence was enough.

Twenty-five years later I still cry about it—damn cigarettes, damn beer, damn diabetes.

At some point, my manhood will stop dreaming of being a boy and will become a man. My manhood has dreams like I do. Both of us want men we cannot have.

Separation

Mice gnawed their way through processed foods
in the cabinet's top shelf—celebration or grief
I'm reminded of those wedding portraits or

wedding cake statues of mice as bride and groom
They don't look happy—never smile—just stand
with whiskers and tails erect at the gallows of matrimony

Perhaps that's why they attended this banquet
traipsing the wildflowers lining the cabinet shelves
exchanging handshakes with their tails

in confirmation or consolation
daily feasts to mourn that house's return
to ashes—marriage's return to dust

I swung at every mouse I could with a corn broom
without cheese or trap—just fury
swept their ineptitude away with mine

None would jump the broom this time
yet others kept coming
They all knew it was done

Briefcase of Little Tortures

Do you remember my first one
I was the scalpel's leather coat on the warmest
[day nobody cares about] after our careless season

I chose to cradle the afterbirth
from my own blood rather than worship
the glory of donating yours

I am gathering in my body a briefcase of little
tortures for you and hoping they are just that
each one a brief case

***

Our first time was like a first night in prison
The rapists and murderers waited to
get a whiff of the Eden in our wandering bones

You were that African girl brought in
to the captain of the slave ship in Roots
eyes cold like post-op Pecola Breedlove

skin cold like pre-op Pecola Breedlove
lying flat, palms like hands up / don't shoot
If Pecola breed love, then I breed lust

and you bleed the bluest cry from the curse
and the seed awaits a whiff of Eve's last fruit
she'd ever really taste

***

I can't look at my four heart chambers
in the photograph anymore without
hearing the song of mirrors in their flesh

I swallow each note with a razor blade
Mama says, They'll come to you when they ready
Ready is sealed in a black Samsonite briefcase

***

I write decaying organs now
Each one dies inside me before
Mama has time to plan the wake
A sharp pain here and there is another word
on the obituary mourning as the
vocabulary becomes more advanced

weeping above you and me
and all those nobodies we used to know
who will sit in the pews and

read this like a love song to death
It's really my final attempt to
pack the briefcase you pray to leave behind

Len Lawson earned a B.S. in Business Administration (Management option) from Winthrop University and an M.A. in English from National University. He has been accepted to the Ph.D. in English Literature & Criticism program at Indiana University of Pennsylvania. He currently teaches writing and literature at Central Carolina Technical College. His scholarly article "Back to the Future: Approaches to Best Practices in Reflective Teaching" appeared in *Cultivating Visionary Leadership by Learning for Global Success: Beyond the Language and Literature Classroom* (Cambridge Scholars Publishing, 2015). He is a Poetry Reader and Book Reviewer for *Up the Staricase Quarterly*.

Len is co-founder of the Poets Respond to Race initiative and co-editor of its upcoming first anthology (Muddy Ford Press). He is a Pushcart Prize nominee, a three-time *Best of the Net* nominee, and a 2016 Callaloo Fellow. He won the 2016 *Jasper Magazine* Artist of the Year Award in Literary Arts. He has been a finalist for the inaugural Berfrois Poetry Prize, the *Mississippi Review* Poetry Prize, and the *Yellow Chair Review* Chapbook Prize. His poetry has also been and will be featured in coffee shops and transit buses in the Columbia, SC metro area, selected by Columbia Poet Laureate Ed Madden.

He has poems appearing or forthcoming in several anthologies and journals including *Callaloo*, *[PANK]*, *The James Franco Review*, *Winter Tangerine Review*, *Pittsburgh Poetry Review*, and *Charleston Currents*, selected by South Carolina Poet Laureate Marjory Wentworth. His website is www.lenlawson.co.

www.ingramcontent.com/pod-product-compliance
Lightning Source LLC
LaVergne TN
LVHW041552070426
835507LV00011B/1052